NEW ORLEANS
CLASSICS

TROMBONE
SOLO

MUSIC MINUS ONE

3934

SUGGESTIONS FOR USING THIS MMO EDITION

WE HAVE TRIED to create a product that will provide you an easy way to learn and perform these compositions with a full ensemble in the comfort of your own home. Because it involves a fixed accompaniment performance, there is an inherent lack of flexibility in tempo. The following MMO features and techniques will reduce these inflexibilities and help you maximize the effectiveness of the MMO practice and performance system:

We have observed generally accepted tempi, and always in the originally intended key, but some may wish to perform at a different tempo, or to slow down or speed up the accompaniment for practice purposes; or to alter the piece to a more comfortable key. We have included slow-tempo versions of the most up-tempo pieces on this album for practice and/or a slower interpretation. But for even more flexibility, you can purchase from MMO specialized CD players & recorders which allow variable speed while maintaining proper pitch, and vice versa. This is an indispensable tool for the serious musician and you may wish to look into purchasing this useful piece of equipment for full enjoyment of all your MMO editions.

We want to provide you with the most useful practice and performance accompaniments possible. If you have any suggestions for improving the MMO system, please feel free to contact us. You can reach us by e-mail at info@musicminusone.com.

3934

CONTENTS

COMPLETE VERSION TRACK DISC A	MINUS VERSION TRACK DISC A/B	SLOW MINUS TRACK DISC B		PAGE
	11 A 1 B		*Tuning Notes*	
1	12 A	❿	*Fidgety Feet*	4
2	13 A		*Tin Roof Blues*	6
3	2 B	⓫	*Royal Garden Blues*	8
4	3 B		*Blue Orleans*	10
5	4 B	⓬	*Dumaine Street Breakdown*	12
6	5 B		*Savoy Blues*	14
7	6 B		*March of the Uncle Bubbys*	16
8	7 B		*Do You Know What It Means to Miss New Orleans?*	18
9	8 B		*Someday You'll Be Sorry*	20
10	9 B	⓭	*Quincy Street Stomp*	22

ISBN 1-59615-110-0

Fidgety Feet

Original Dixieland Jazz Band

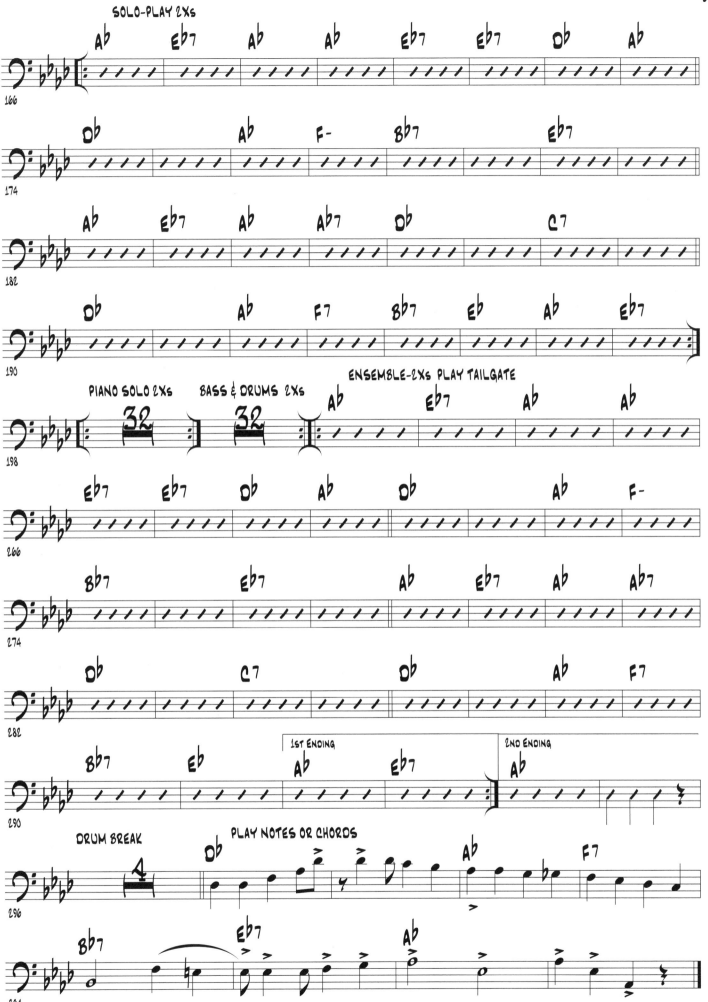

Trombone

Tin Roof Blues

New Orleans Rhythm Kings

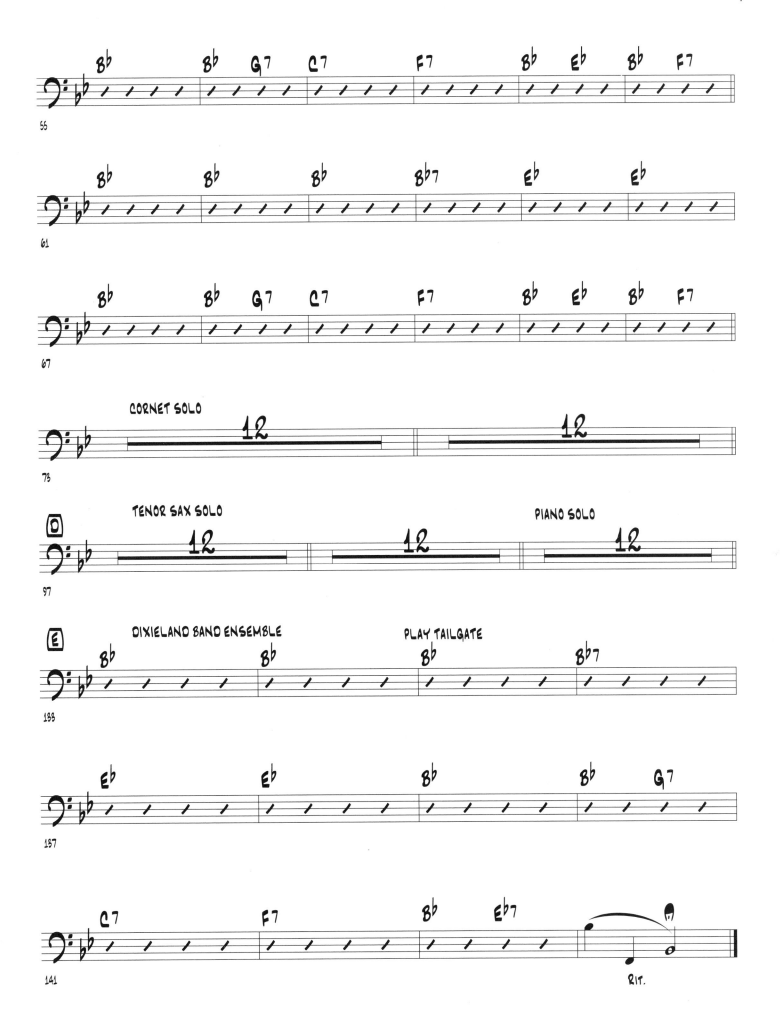

Royal Garden Blues

Clarence & Spencer Williams

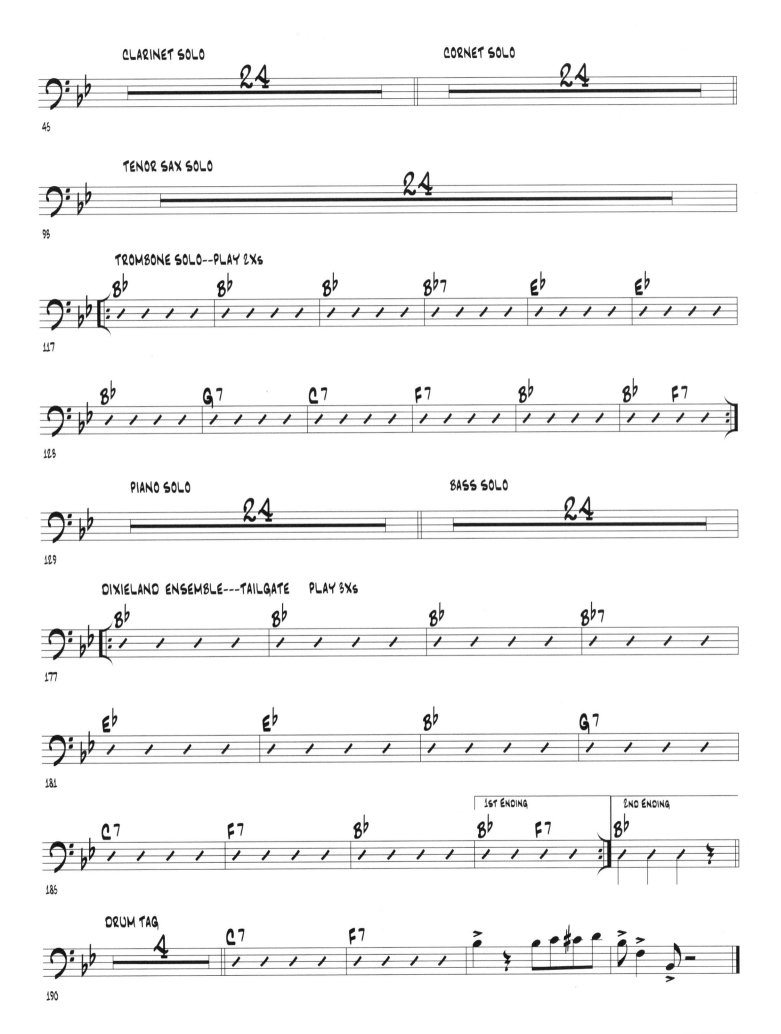

Trombone

Blue Orleans

Tim Laughlin

Dumaine Street Breakdown

Trombone

Tim Laughlin

MMO 3934

Trombone

Savoy Blues

Edward "Kid" Ory

MMO 3934

Trombone

March of the Uncle Bubbys

Tim Laughlin

Trombone

Do You Know What It Means to Miss New Orleans?

Eddie DeLang
Louis Alter

Trombone

Someday You'll Be Sorry

DIXIELAND BAND-ENSEMBLE-PLAY TAILGATE

Louis Armstrong

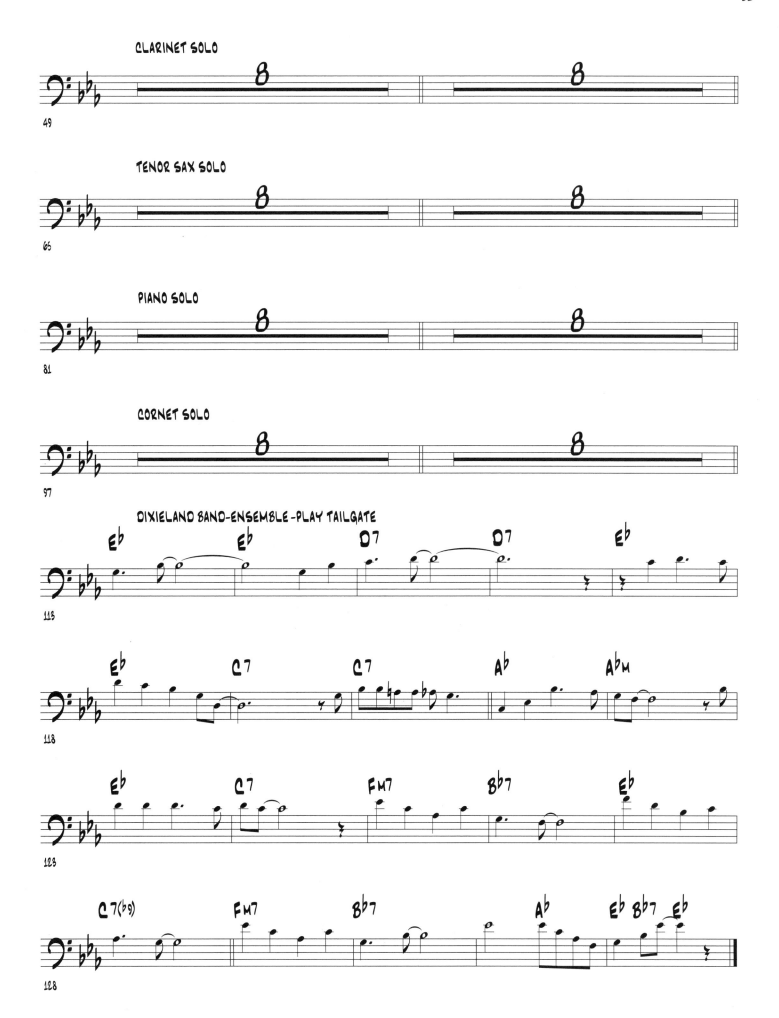

Quincy Street Stomp

Sidney Bechet

MMO 3934

MUSIC MINUS ONE

50 Executive Boulevard
Elmsford, New York 10523-1325
1.800.669.7464 (U.S.)/914.592.1188 (International)

www.musicminusone.com
e-mail: mmogroup@musicminusone.com

MMO 3934   Pub. No. 00264   Printed in Canada